WILLIAM MORRIS
IN 50 OBJECTS

Carien Kremer and Anna Mason

William Morris Gallery
Lloyd Park
Forest Road
Walthamstow
London E17 4PP

Tel 020 8496 4390
www.wmgallery.org.uk

Waltham Forest

*'With the arrogance of youth,
I determined to do no less than to
transform the world with Beauty.'*

Introduction

William Morris rebelled against the age in which he lived. Not only a pioneer of pattern, he made original contributions to poetry, design, craft, politics and conservation. His deep sympathy for the medieval past inspired him to re-imagine the future creatively. Morris was a practical reformer who pursued his ideals with relentless energy. What constitutes a meaningful life? What is the secret to human happiness? What is the purpose of art? These are some of the questions that Morris tried to address over the course of a full and varied career. When he died at the age of sixty-two, one doctor stated that 'the disease is simply being William Morris, and having done more work than most ten men'.

William Morris
aged twenty-three

Morris & Co employees hand-knotting a carpet, late 19th century

Morris revolutionised British design and his ideas continue to inspire successive generations of artists. He promoted functional design, sympathetic use of natural materials and, above all, high standards of craftsmanship. In 1861, together with a group of friends, he founded the interior design business Morris, Marshall, Faulkner & Company, known affectionately as 'the Firm'. The partners claimed to offer an alternative to the shoddy, mass-produced wares of industrial Britain. Describing themselves as 'Artists of reputation', they provided a complete design service, from wall decoration to stained glass and furniture.

The Firm's partners made an impressive line-up. Ford Madox Brown and Dante Gabriel Rossetti were already painters of reputation. Edward Burne-Jones, Morris's closest university friend and lifelong collaborator, was a painter with experience of designing stained glass. The architect Philip Webb had established his reputation with his design for Morris's first marital home, Red House in Bexleyheath. At first, Morris was one of the least experienced artists in the group, but ultimately it was his drive and determination that would bring the business international renown.

When the Firm was launched in the 1860s, it had long been recognised that standards of design in Britain needed reform. Over the coming decades, Morris's unique contribution was his fanatical interest in how things were made. Where he found contemporary manufacturing processes flawed, he revived ancient craft techniques in his relentless pursuit for quality. He looked to other cultures for inspiration — particularly the Middle East and the Indian subcontinent. A recognised expert on historic textiles, he was also a practitioner. Whether it was carpet knotting or tapestry weaving, he first mastered the technique himself before introducing it to his workshops. This hands-on approach was unusual amongst designers at the time.

Why was hand-craftsmanship so important to Morris? It stemmed from his belief that Victorian society had lost its way. To turn a quick profit, large factories were mass-producing poorly made goods, recklessly encouraging a culture of throwaway consumerism. He witnessed the devastating impact of industrialisation on both the landscape and the lives of factory workers. In his own business, he tried a different approach. His workshops at Merton Abbey in Surrey were small scale. The rural environment was pleasant and his employees worked reasonable hours for an above-average wage. Apprentices were trained in a specialist craft skill, be it dyeing or tapestry weaving, and goods were designed to last. Whilst the situation still fell short of Morris's ideal, namely that every worker should be free to explore his or her own creativity, it was a vast improvement on the status quo at the time.

Merton Abbey workshops, late 19th century

MORRIS & COMPANY DECORATORS

449

Morris & Co's Oxford
Street showroom, c.1911

The skilled, labour-intensive techniques that Morris revived made competitive pricing challenging but the Firm still found a growing market for their goods. In 1875 the business was reorganised under Morris's sole control and renamed Morris & Co. The showroom was relocated from Queen Square in Bloomsbury to Oxford Street, a more fashionable West End address. Agents were appointed in the United States and the Firm gradually built up an international reputation. Morris's business acumen is often underestimated, as is the extent to which he came to rely on the profits from Morris & Co. to support his family. As a young man he had the luxury of a private income but when this dried up, his business became his livelihood.

Photograph taken during May Morris's tour of Iceland, 1930s

Morris wrote poetry for pleasure and always pursued his literary interests alongside his design work; he once remarked, 'if a chap can't compose an epic poem while he's weaving a tapestry, he had better shut up, he'll never do any good at all'. *The Earthly Paradise* was his most popular poetic work and became an instant bestseller. It drew on his love of myth and legend, including the Norse and Icelandic sagas. Wishing to experience these stories in their original language, Morris started to learn Old Icelandic. Whenever he acquired a new interest he pursued it with undaunted enthusiasm. With the help of an Icelandic scholar, he translated and published the sagas in English. In the early 1870s he travelled to Iceland, visiting the saga sites and experiencing the barren wildness of the landscape, untainted by industrialisation. Many years later, his daughter May Morris retraced his steps.

Morris returned from his travels more acutely aware of the shortcomings in his own society. Life in Iceland was hard but he admired the resourcefulness of the people and the community spirit, 'the most grinding poverty is a trifling evil compared to the inequality of the classes'. One of the earliest signs of his growing radicalism was his role in the foundation of the Society for the Protection of Ancient Buildings in 1877. This pressure group was created to watch over historic buildings, protecting them from over-zealous restoration. It operated on the assumption that everyone, including future generations, had a stake in historic buildings. Today, this idea of shared heritage is widely accepted. At the time, it was a daring attack on the rights of private property.

In the early 1880s, Morris crossed the 'river of fire' and became a revolutionary socialist. He campaigned to end the capitalist system and sweep away the privileges enjoyed by his own class. Always a man of action, he threw himself into the task, giving outdoor speeches, attending rallies and publishing radical newspapers. He continued to run his design business but poured much of the profit back into his political activities. Reforming the decorative arts and bringing about social change were closely-related ambitions. In the society of the future, he hoped that everyone would live in comfortable, pleasant surroundings and enjoy creative manual work. Only under these conditions would the arts flourish: 'I do not want art for a few, any more than education for a few, or freedom for a few'.

Gathering of the Hammersmith
Socialist League, 1889

Water House in the 19th century

William Morris and Walthamstow

William Morris was born in Walthamstow in 1834, then 'one of the largest and handsomest suburban villages near the metropolis...[containing] many large villas, with tasteful pleasure grounds'. The eldest son of a successful City financier, Morris spent his childhood exploring Epping Forest and the Essex countryside. Over the years, the family leased several properties in the area but the only one to escape demolition was Water House, now home to the William Morris Gallery.

Constructed in the 1740s, this fine Georgian villa was originally of square proportions. By 1758 it had been substantially enlarged with the addition of two flanking wings. The original east wing, demolished c.1900, once housed the kitchens and servants' accommodation. Throughout most of its history as a private house, the property was leased to affluent tenants. To appeal to this market, successive owners carried out improvements and modernisations. The most dramatic change was the remodelling of the front façade in the second half of the 18th century. The addition of full-height, semicircular bays and the Corinthian columned timber porch added a sense of grandeur to this elevation.

Morris's connection with Water House began in 1848, when he was fourteen years old. Recently widowed with nine children to support, his mother gave up a lease on Woodford Hall, a large mansion on the edge of Epping Forest. Smaller, though still impressive, Water House was home to the family until 1856. It was the grounds, particularly the moated island and kitchen gardens, that made the greatest impression on the young William Morris. The brothers fished or swam in the moat and the island itself was 'a sort of fairyland for all the children, who almost lived on it'.

After the Morris tenancy ended, the property was purchased by the publisher Edward Lloyd (1815–1890). As a young man, Lloyd sold cheap popular literature, plagiarising the work of famous authors, including Charles Dickens. His business tactics were unscrupulous but effective. A successful newspaper magnate, he slashed prices and dramatically increased circulation. Lloyd fathered twenty-one children, and with the addition of servants the house must have felt rather cramped despite its generous proportions.

The Lloyd family at Water House, 1860s

Water House becomes a public gallery

In 1899, the Lloyd family donated the house and grounds to the people of Walthamstow. The grounds were swiftly transformed into a park, opening to the public in 1900. The future of the house was more uncertain. The Lloyd family had moved away in 1885 and since then the building had fallen into disrepair. As early as 1908 there was local interest in creating a museum dedicated to Morris, but as yet no collection to display. Plans to convert the building into a school were abandoned but for many years it served as a dental surgery. The turning point came in the 1930s. Local celebrations for the centenary of Morris's birth renewed interest in plans to create a museum. Soon afterwards, the local council was offered two important collections of art — the Brangwyn Gift and the Mackmurdo Bequest.

Sir Frank Brangwyn R.A. (1867–1956) served a brief apprenticeship with Morris & Co. as a young man. Although he left to pursue a career as a painter, he later developed a strong interest in the decorative arts. Brangwyn subscribed to Morris's belief that art should exist for everyone, not just the privileged few. Encouraged by the local artist, Walter Spradbery, his gift to Walthamstow included some of his greatest oils, mural designs, prints and watercolours. Brangwyn also donated paintings and sculpture by a wide range of mainly 19th century British and Continental artists, including significant works by the Pre-Raphaelite Brotherhood.

The architect and designer Arthur Heygate Mackmurdo (1851–1942) was also persuaded to make a generous bequest. Mackmurdo founded the Century Guild in the 1880s, a short-lived but influential Arts and Crafts organisation. The Gallery's holdings include the world's most comprehensive collection of Century Guild designs, textiles, wallpapers and furniture as well as important archival material.

From left to right:
Spradbery, Brangwyn and Mackmurdo, 1939

These gifts were supplemented by Morris material gathered by the Walthamstow Antiquarian Society since 1914. When Morris & Co. ceased trading in 1940, original working drawings and remaining stock were also acquired for the new museum. Plans were shelved during the Second World War but in 1950 the Gallery finally opened its doors to the public. The Prime Minister and local M.P. Clement Attlee presided over the opening ceremony.

Since 1950, the collections have continued to expand and new acquisitions are still made today. The holdings are uniquely placed to tell the full story of this fascinating and unusually energetic man and his artistic circle. Work by younger designers within the Arts and Crafts Movement is also well represented: in addition to the Century Guild collections there are significant works by May Morris, George Jack and Christopher Whall, to name but a few.

Image by Pringle Richards Sharratt Architects

The William Morris Gallery today

In 2012 the Gallery entered a new phase in its history. An ambitious redevelopment has restored the Grade II* listed Georgian building with the construction of a new extension designed by Pringle Richards Sharratt Architects. The collection has been redisplayed and new learning and research facilities have been created to encourage wider engagement with Morris and his continuing legacy. The displays are regularly rotated and complemented by an exciting programme of special exhibitions, activities and events so there is always something new to see and discover.

Waltham Forest Council has been the driving force behind this redevelopment, which has been generously supported by the Heritage Lottery Fund, The Friends of the William Morris Gallery, and numerous trusts, foundations and individual donors, without whom the project would not have been possible and to whom we are most grateful.

This pocket guide presents a glimpse of the richness of the Morris collections at the William Morris Gallery. Fifty objects have been selected to illustrate the breadth of his achievements and those of his closest collaborators. We hope that you will enjoy this book and that it will also be the catalyst for you to come and visit the William Morris Gallery and see the collections beautifully presented in his childhood home.

Water House, Walthamstow, c.1860s

When William Morris's father died in 1847, his mother moved to a smaller house that was easier to manage. She chose a three-storey Georgian villa with stables, kitchen gardens and pleasure grounds comprising eight acres. The grounds had their own island surrounded by the moat that gave the property its name.

The Morris family lived here from 1848 to 1856. During this time William attended boarding school and later Oxford University. He came home in the holidays, fishing in the moat and exploring nearby Epping Forest. He also invited his lifelong friend, the painter Edward Burne-Jones: 'Three happy days they spent together, talking as they wandered about the flower and high-walled kitchen gardens, or reading in the deep window seats of a landing on the big central staircase, where many books were kept'.

This photograph shows later residents, the Lloyd family, who lived at Water House from 1857 to 1885. The extension to the left with the tall chimney once housed the kitchens and the servants' quarters. Today, Water House is home to the William Morris Gallery.

hand-coloured photograph, 7.5 x 7.7 cm

William Morris, c.1870s

Morris had an unconventional dress sense. At university he went through a phase of wearing purple trousers. Later his shirts and jackets were made almost exclusively from cloth dyed his favourite colour — indigo blue. The novelist Henry James described him as 'short, burly, corpulent, very careless and unfinished in his dress'. His unruly hair and scruffy appearance sometimes led to mistaken identity. Servants were known to refuse him entry when he called at the great houses of his clients and one shop assistant reported him as a 'suspicious character' before realising his mistake.

As his scowl suggests, Morris disliked being photographed and only cooperated under duress. His willingness to wear a working smock in the photograph reveals a great deal about his attitude to manual labour. Unlike many design reformers, he was a hands-on craftsman. In Victorian Britain even skilled manual work was shunned by the educated classes. Morris, in flouting this convention, was making a radical social statement.

photograph, 9 x 6 cm

'You see I do not hope to be great at all in anything, but perhaps I may reasonably hope to be happy in my work…'

'My dear Mother…'

Morris and Burne-Jones both planned to pursue a career in the church. This respectable occupation was looked upon favourably by Morris's mother who had high ambitions for her eldest son. However, at university the two friends discovered art and literature and became disillusioned with the Ministry.

At first, Morris decided to become an architect. It is clear from this letter that his mother did not take the news well. 'You said then, you remember, and said very truly, that it was an evil thing to be an idle, objectless man'. Morris went to great lengths to justify his decision, reassuring his mother that architecture is 'a useful trade, one by which I should hope to earn money'.

Earlier that year Morris had inherited a private income from his father's estate. The family's wealth derived from lucrative mining shares and this financial independence gave Morris the freedom to make his own decisions. Although he soon gave up his architectural ambitions, he remained committed to an artistic life.

William Morris to Emma Shelton Morris, 11 November 1855

Ex: Coll: Oxon
Nov. 11th 1855

My dear Mother

I am almost afraid you thought
me scarcely in earnest when I told you
a month or two ago that I did not intend
taking Holy orders; if this is the case I am
afraid also that my letter now may vex
you; but if you have really made up
your mind that I was in earnest. I think
you will be pleased with my resolution.
You said then, you remember, and said
very truly, that it was an evil thing
to be an idle, objectless man; I am
fully determined not to incur this reproach,
I was so then though I did not tell you
at the time all I thought of,
partly because I had not thought about
it enough myself, and partly because I
wished to give you time to become reconciled
to the idea of my continuing a lay person

West Porch of Rouen Cathedral, unknown date

John Ruskin, the most influential art critic of the Victorian era, called upon his readers to 'go forth again to gaze upon the old cathedral front…examine once more those ugly goblins, and formless monsters, and stern statues…but do not mock at them, for they are signs of the life and liberty of every workman who struck the stone'.

Morris was heavily influenced by Ruskin, discovering his work whilst at university. Ruskin's praise for Gothic architecture and his criticism of Victorian industrialisation struck a chord with Morris. He followed Ruskin's advice and travelled to Northern France with Burne-Jones, visiting the cathedrals of Chartres, Amiens and Rouen. During this trip, enthused by the medieval architecture, the friends decided to devote their lives to art.

This detailed drawing, attributed to Ruskin or one of his assistants, was probably created to record the appearance of the medieval fabric of the Cathedral when it was threatened by over-zealous restoration. Rouen remained important to Morris and a year before he died he protested against the threat to this 'most beautiful monument of art'.

pencil, sepia wash and watercolour on paper, 76.2 x 62.3 cm

Tub chair, c.1861

Morris discovered his talents as a designer almost by accident. In 1856, he moved into shared London lodgings with Burne-Jones in Red Lion Square, Holborn. The rooms had formerly been let by the Pre-Raphaelite painter, Dante Gabriel Rossetti, who was already mentoring Burne-Jones in his efforts to become a painter. The lodgings were unfurnished and with typical enthusiasm Morris designed his own furniture. The construction was entrusted to a local carpenter and the friends hand-painted each piece.

This solid, deliberately unsophisticated, chair is characteristic of Morris's early attempts to emulate the Gothic style. The back panels are painted with stylised bird and plant motifs in deep greens, reds and blues. In addition to the heavy furniture, the rooms were decorated with brass rubbings, antique metalwork and ceramics that he purchased on his travels in France and Belgium.

Morris was always an independent spirit and the furnishings at Red Lion Square were a deliberate rejection of mainstream Victorian design. His antipathy to industrial manufacture was evident even as a teenager when he refused to visit the Great Exhibition of 1851, describing this hugely popular event as 'wonderfully ugly'.

ebonised and painted wood, 63 x 75 x 51.5 cm

Jane in medieval costume, 1861

Jane Burden was an unconventional beauty. The daughter of an Oxford stable-hand, she was raised from obscurity when her looks caught the attention of Morris's friends. After some persuasion, she began to work as an artist's model and her long wavy hair, full mouth and sorrowful expression feature in many paintings, particularly the works of Rossetti.

Morris, whose previous experience of women seems to have been very limited, quickly fell in love. With complete disregard for their different social backgrounds, the couple married in 1859. The following year they moved to Red House in Bexleyheath, designed by Morris's close friend Philip Webb.

Morris and his fellow artists decorated the house with murals, painted patterns and embroidered hangings. They created a unique interior, fashioned by hand and owing nothing to industrial design. A painted mural depicting the Siege of Troy was planned for the stairwell. Morris's drawing of Jane about to board a ship is possibly a study of Helen of Troy for this wall painting. Jane was talented at needlework and probably made the costume herself. Morris's interest in pattern is already evident in the ornate lining of the sleeve.

pencil and ink on paper, 51 x 41 cm

Embroidered hanging, c.1861

Embroidery was the first of the textile arts that Morris explored. In the early days of their marriage at Red House, Morris and Jane worked on embroidery together. They unpicked examples of old work that they admired to learn the different stitch techniques.

This hanging was designed by Morris and typifies the experimental, non-commercial and intensely medieval characteristics of his early work. The tree, banner and bird motif was inspired by an illustration in a medieval manuscript that he was studying at the time. The French inscription is taken from Geoffrey Chaucer's poem *Parliament of Fowls* and translates as he 'who loves best loves longest'.

The embroidery was one of a set of identical hangings installed at Penkill Castle, Ayrshire, by the late 1860s. This property belonged to Alice Boyd, mistress of the painter William Bell Scott, who was closely connected to Rossetti and the Pre-Raphaelite circle. The design probably dates to the Red House period in the first half of the 1860s. The densely stitched background deliberately evokes the medieval tapestries that Morris so admired.

wools embroidered on a linen ground, 185.5 x 127.5 cm

Acquired with the assistance of the MGC /V&A Purchase Grant Fund and Friends of the WMG.

Labours of the Months, c.1862

The experience of furnishing Red House inspired Morris and his friends to establish a decorating business. In 1861, they founded Morris, Marshall, Faulkner & Company. This group of 'Fine Art Workmen' offered to undertake every kind of interior decoration. Hand-painted tiles were among their earliest products.

This tile series represents the twelve months of the year. It largely follows the medieval convention of depicting each month with an appropriate agricultural task. July is symbolised by a labourer gathering hay and September by a woman pressing grapes for wine. Other months have different attributes. January is represented by the Roman god Janus and in February a woman reads a love letter in reference to St Valentine.

Burne-Jones, Morris, Rossetti and Ford Madox Brown all contributed designs for this series. The signs of the zodiac were supplied by Webb, who for Aquarius drew an affectionate caricature of Morris. Lucy Faulkner, sister of one of the partners, painted many early tiles and the border of the February panel bears her initials 'LJF'.

hand-painted on tin-glazed earthenware tiles,
12.7 x 12.7 cm each tile

Acquired with the assistance of the MGC/V&A Purchase Grant Fund, National Heritage Memorial Fund, Friends of the WMG and Walthamstow Historical Society.

Trellis wallpaper design, 1862

Trellis was the first wallpaper Morris designed. He took inspiration from the rose trellises in his garden at Red House. Close inspection of this original design reveals areas that have been altered as Morris worked out the structure of the pattern. The key lines were then finalised in ink. Webb, who drew the animals for several of Morris's designs, added the flying birds. The coloured squares test out different background colours and the design was eventually printed in several colourways.

Morris first tried to print the paper himself, using zinc plates and oil-based inks. Disappointed with the results, he turned to Jeffrey & Co, a reputable wallpaper manufacturer who used the standard woodblock printing process. From this moment on, Jeffrey & Co. printed all the Firm's wallpapers to an extremely high standard.

pencil, ink and watercolour on paper, 66 x 61 cm

Slaying of the Lord's Son, c.1861–62

Stained glass was one of the Firm's most important early products, partly owing to the rapid growth of new churches. This development was encouraged by religious reform, growing urban populations and wealth generated by industrial production and trade. It provided a profitable market for church furnishings and contributed to the Firm's early success.

This stained glass design by Rossetti was one of a series illustrating the biblical Parable of the Vineyard. In this scene, a landlord returns home to find that his son has been murdered by his greedy tenants. The men in armour try to batter down the door to punish them, whilst the landlord grieves for his son.

The stained glass panels created from these designs were exhibited at the International Exhibition of 1862. The Firm's stand received mixed reviews but succeeded in attracting new business. The stained glass in particular was singled out for its 'artistic qualities of colour and design'. Until 1865, the Firm's workshop was located at 8 Red Lion Square and apprentices were recruited from the nearby Industrial Home for Destitute Boys in Euston.

grey wash, charcoal and white bodycolour on paper,
60.9 x 91.4 cm

Acquired with the assistance of the V&A Purchase Grant Fund.

*'a jewel-like quality is the
chief charm of painted glass'*

Minstrel with Cymbals, 1880s

The Firm's partners were paid a fee for every design they produced. Designs were precious assets and were often re-used or adapted for subsequent commissions. Morris designed this figure in 1868 and it was used repeatedly in both domestic and religious buildings. The minstrel could become an angel by simply adding wings, making it a suitable choice for church commissions. The design was also adapted for tiles and embroidery.

As well as contributing designs, Morris played a vital role in the production of stained glass windows. He took responsibility for placing the lead-lines, choosing the colours and supervising the assembly. The deep jewel-like colours were inspired by the best examples of medieval glass and carefully selected to harmonise together.

The Firm bought most of its glass from James Powell & Sons and never manufactured its own. Morris often used glass that was coloured all the way through and had interesting tonal variations that could be used to great effect in the design. Other details were added by painting onto the surface of the glass.

stained, painted and leaded glass, 64.5 x 47.5 cm

Acquired with the assistance of the MGC/V&A Purchase Grant Fund, The Art Fund, Friends of the WMG, the Bancroft's and West Essex Decorative & Fine Art Societies.

Beauty and the Beast, c.1863–64

In the 1860s Burne-Jones designed a number of tile panels depicting folktales for the house of the watercolourist Myles Birket Foster. This panel decorated one of the bedroom fireplaces. The inscription reads: 'How a Prince who by enchantment was under the form of a beast became a man again by the love of a certain maiden'. Burne-Jones is thought to have based his design for the beast on a bear that Webb sketched at London Zoo.

The style is deliberately child-like to reflect the subject matter. The design also recalls the influence of the German print-maker Ludwig Richter, whose work Burne-Jones admired. The final panel was a collaborative effort: Morris designed the blue and white swan motif and Lucy Faulkner painted the tiles.

hand-painted on tin-glazed earthenware tiles,
15.2 x 15.2 cm each tile

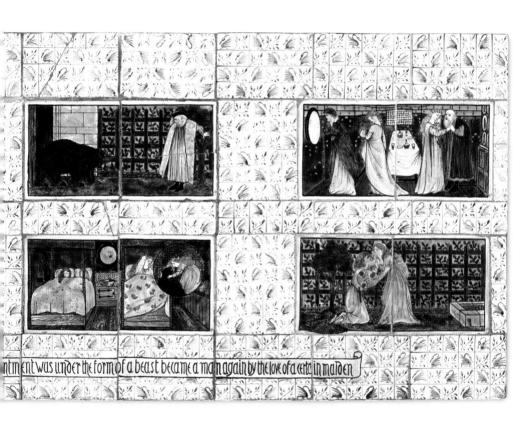

ntment was under the form of a beast became a man again by the love of a certain maiden

The God of Love and Alceste, c.1864

Morris and Burne-Jones regarded Chaucer as the greatest writer of the medieval age. They returned to his stories time and time again, sharing and re-telling them in new ways.

The Legend of Good Women inspired this stained glass window designed by Burne-Jones. In Chaucer's tale, the winged God of Love and his wife Alceste reprimand the poet for depicting women in a bad light. They demand a poem celebrating the virtues of women throughout history. What actually follows is an account of various mythical women, not all virtuous, many of whom have suffered for love.

The poem had already inspired Morris's ambitious decorative scheme for the dining room at Red House. Although never completed, he planned a series of large embroidered hangings depicting different heroines. The theme reappears in another embroidery scheme that Burne-Jones designed for Ruskin in the early 1860s.

stained, painted and leaded glass, 63 x 74 cm

Purchased with support from the MGC/V&A Purchase Grant Fund, The Art Fund, the Friends of the WMG and the West Essex Decorative & Fine Art Society.

Eve and the Virgin, designed 1864

In the early years of the Firm, all the partners contributed designs for stained glass. This life-size cartoon was devised by Morris for the chancel east window in the church of All Saints, Middleton Cheney in Northamptonshire.

The figures have been pasted down onto a decorative background of fruit trees. Eve carries a distaff or spinning tool under her arm and is heavily draped in animal skins and fur. She has already succumbed to temptation in the Garden of Eden and lowers her eyes in shame. The Virgin walks with her head up holding a lily, the traditional symbol of purity. The two figures represent the religious tradition that Mary's absolute virtue counteracts Eve's 'original sin'.

This working drawing was a preliminary step in creating the finished panel. There are small colour notations on the Virgin's robe and the positioning of the lead lines still had to be worked out before the glass could be selected and cut to size.

sepia wash and pencil on paper, 74.9 x 55.9 cm

Saint George and the Dragon, 1868

Inspired by the legend of Saint George, this painting by Burne-Jones depicts the moment when George slays the dragon. This act liberates the pagan Princess Sabra, who has been offered as a sacrifice to protect her father's city. Dressed in white and tied to a stake, she is a diminutive figure in the distance. George and the dragon gaze almost sorrowfully at one another — a lyrical treatment of a potentially dramatic and violent subject.

The legend of Saint George had already inspired decorative work by the Firm, including painted furniture and stained glass. Burne-Jones had also completed a series of oil paintings on the legend for the dining room of Birket Foster. This smaller, watercolour version was made later and the composition has been altered.

The reflection of light on the Saint's armour and the dragon's scales has been expertly achieved and the work is sometimes mistaken for an oil painting. Burne-Jones perfected a technique of using thick layers of watercolour and gouache to simulate the texture and luminosity of oil.

watercolour and gouache on paper, 62 x 48 cm

Conserved with the assistance of The Radcliffe Trust.

Michael Scott's Wooing, c.1870

Rossetti played a crucial role in the Firm's early success. A founding member of the Pre-Raphaelite Brotherhood, he had already achieved recognition as both a painter and poet. The Firm won some of its earliest commissions through his contacts.

This chalk study depicts the medieval Scottish magician and astronomer Michael Scott placing a ring on the finger of a young girl. The model was Jane Morris, with whom Rossetti was having an affair. The winged figure of love looks up, away from the couple and a draped woman cuts a cross from the girl's girdle.

There was never an open rift in Morris's marriage although he was clearly hurt by the betrayal. His relationship with Rossetti naturally became increasingly strained. In 1875 Morris reorganised the Firm under his sole control and, after some disputes, bought out the original partners, including Rossetti.

red and black chalk on paper, 73 x 75.6 cm

Sussex chair range, c.1911

The Firm's iconic rush-seated chairs first appeared in the 1860s and this catalogue from 1911 shows the full range. The advertisement readily admits that the design was copied 'with trifling improvements' from a country chair, but also acknowledges its continuing popularity.

Warrington Taylor, the Firm's first business manager, summed up the chair's appeal: 'essentially gentlemanly with a total absence of ex-tallow chandler vulgarity – it possesses poetry of simplicity'. Taylor recognised the commercial potential. The light and elegant chairs could be held in stock and sold at a relatively affordable price.

However, even these simple chairs could be adapted for special customers. A 'Sussex single chair' in the collection was painted dark green for the artist and patron George Howard, 9th Earl of Carlisle, one of the Firm's most important clients. The chairs were also popular with the Firm's partners who all used them at home.

THE SUSSEX RUSH-SEATED CHAIRS
MORRIS AND COMPANY
449 OXFORD STREET, LONDON, W.

"ROSSETTI" ARM-CHAIR.
IN BLACK, 16/6.

SUSSEX CORNER CHAIR.
IN BLACK, 10/6.

SUSSEX SINGLE CHAIR.
IN BLACK, 7/-.

SUSSEX ARM-CHAIR.
IN BLACK, 9/9.

ROUND-SEAT CHAIR.
IN BLACK, 10/6.

SUSSEX SETTEE, 4 FT. 6 IN. LONG.
IN BLACK, 35/-.

ROUND SEAT PIANO CHAIR.
IN BLACK, 10/6.

"Of all the specific minor improvements in common household objects due to Morris, the rush-bottomed Sussex chair perhaps takes the first place. It was not his own invention, but was copied with trifling improvements from an old chair of village manufacture picked up in Sussex. With or without modification it has been taken up by all the modern furniture manufacturers, and is in almost universal use. But the Morris pattern of the later type (there were two) still excels all others in simplicity and elegance of proportion."

"*Life of William Morris*": *By Prof. J. W. Mackail.*

63

Zephyr and Psyche, c.1866–68

Morris was most famous in his own lifetime as a poet. His experiments in writing verse began at university. *The Earthly Paradise* was his most celebrated work — an epic re-telling of ancient stories, from the Icelandic sagas to the legends of Classical Greece and Rome.

As Morris wrote *The Earthly Paradise*, he 'saw the stories in brilliantly defined pictures, and desired that other people should do so too'. He set out to produce a fully illustrated edition of his poem and enlisted Burne-Jones to design the woodcut illustrations. Unfortunately this project proved too ambitious and the illustrated version never appeared. A number of the trial wood engravings survive and give a wonderful glimpse of the 'book that never was'.

This illustration was designed for the legend of Cupid and Psyche. It shows Zephyr, the god of the wind, carrying the sleeping Psyche far above her father's castle to the land of the gods.

wood engraving on paper, 15.1 x 10.6 cm

Acquired with the assistance of the V&A Purchase Grant Fund.

Morris and Burne-Jones families, 1874

The two families pose together for the celebrated photographer, Frederick Hollyer. Jenny Morris, the elder daughter, is seated next to Jane. Jenny showed great academic promise before tragically developing epilepsy as a teenager. May Morris, standing next to her father, later became a well-respected embroideress and teacher. Both the girls and Jane wear loose fitting clothes, which was unusual at the time. Morris famously wrote that most Victorian women were 'upholstered like armchairs'.

Burne-Jones holds his daughter Margaret; his son, Philip, and wife, Georgiana, sit in front. The Victorians rarely smiled for the camera, which makes this photograph a bit unnerving for today's audience. The families were very close for over three decades and usually spent Christmas together.

However, when this photograph was taken both couples were having a difficult time. Morris and Georgie were both suffering from their partners' marital infidelities. This shared experience brought them closer together. Around this time, Morris produced illuminated calligraphic manuscripts and several of these were presented as gifts to Georgie.

photograph, 15 x 13.6 cm

Living English Poets, c.1883

The illustrator Walter Crane designed this sketch for the frontispiece to the anthology *Living English Poets*. Morris's work was included in the book together with that of Browning, Swinburne, Arnold, Tennyson and many others.

The sketch shows the poets gathered around a temple dedicated to the British muses. In the finished design these included Chaucer, Shakespeare and Milton. The living poets are thus presented as the successors to these great writers. The seated goddess hands out laurel wreaths, a symbol of literary fame from the Classical world.

Morris is at the front, lying down and holding a copy of *The Earthly Paradise*. In his left hand he clutches some daisies growing in the grass. The flowers symbolise his design work, in which the daisy motif frequently appears. They remind the viewer that Morris was famous for his poetry but equally committed to the decorative arts.

pencil and ink on paper, 18.1 x 13 cm

Adoration of the Magi, 1872

In the 1870s, Burne-Jones became the Firm's chief designer of figurative stained glass. The Adoration of the Magi was one of four panels on the theme of Christ's nativity. Commissioned for the chapel of Castle Howard in Yorkshire, the great stately home of the Earls of Carlisle, the panels remain in situ and can still be visited today.

In this design, Mary holds her newborn son as the three kings approach bearing a gift. Traditionally the kings represented the three continents known to medieval Christendom: Europe, Asia and Africa. The bold, linear treatment of the drapery and the almost sculptural quality of the figures mark a departure from Burne-Jones's designs of the 1860s.

The 9th Earl, George Howard, and his wife were personal friends of the Morris and Burne-Jones families and important patrons of the Firm. They commissioned Webb to design their London home at 1 Palace Green, Kensington, which was lavishly decorated by Morris & Co. and also used the Firm for their ancestral home at Naworth in Cumbria.

watercolour, bodycolour and pencil on paper, 105.5 x 100 cm
Conserved with the assistance of The Mercers' Company.

The Pelican in Her Piety, 1880

The stained glass windows at St Martin's Church in Brampton, Cumbria are one of Morris & Co.'s masterpieces. After the windows were complete, Burne-Jones used coloured chalks to transform his design into this highly finished work.

The pelican feeding its young with drops of blood from its breast is a Christian emblem for the sacrifice of Christ on the cross. The nest sits on top of a highly stylised tree with sinuous curves. In the 20th century, the art historian Nikolaus Pevsner published this design as a precursor of Art Nouveau.

St Martin's Church was designed by Webb under the patronage of the Howard family. Morris wrote to George Howard, expressing his relief 'that you think the east window a success. I was very nervous about it, as the cartoons were so good that I should have been quite upset if I had not done them something like justice'. Burne-Jones felt that he had been underpaid for his contribution and was only half in jest when he referred to the scheme as a 'monument of art and ingratitude'.

pencil, coloured chalk and gold on paper, 172.7 x 57.2 cm

'If you want to be comfortable, go to bed.'

Settle, c.1890s

Morris divided furniture into two categories. 'Necessary work-a-day' furniture ought to be simple and functional, as demonstrated by the Firm's rush-seated chairs. In contrast, more elaborate 'state furniture' was suited for the principal reception rooms of the house. These statement pieces were available by special commission and the design was often adapted to the taste of the client.

This grand settle was designed by Webb in the 1860s. The shallow canopy was deliberately medieval in appearance. The wooden panels have been embellished with gilded plasterwork, showing three infants (known as 'putti' in Classical iconography) roaming among fruit trees. Morris owned an earlier version with more restrained decoration applied to panels of painted leather. The seat was originally fitted with a back cushion so it would have been marginally more comfortable than it appears today.

oak with gilt gesso, seat upholstered in Morris & Co. velvet, 209 x 198 x 56 cm

Design for *African Marigold*, 1876

In his lecture *Some Hints on Pattern Designing*, Morris explained the importance of the decorative arts. He regarded 'beauty' as a basic human need that could only be satisfied by the best possible art. By 'art' he meant not just paintings and sculpture, but the home furnishings that surround us in our everyday life.

Morris's patterns are inspired by natural forms, but he did not see any value in a realistic representation of nature. Instead he wanted to stimulate the imagination, hinting at a world beyond the pattern:

'Is it not better to be reminded, however simply, of the close vine-trellis that keeps out the sun by the Nile side; or of the wild-woods and their streams, with the dogs panting beside them...? Is not all this better than having to count day after day a few sham-real boughs and flowers, casting sham-real shadows on your walls with little hint of anything beyond Covent Garden in them?'

pencil, ink and watercolour on paper, 94.5 x 66.2 cm

Snakeshead, designed 1876

When Morris started to design printed textiles, his showroom manager, George Wardle, advised him to visit his brother-in-law. Thomas Wardle ran a successful silk dyeing and printing business in Leek, Staffordshire. Although his father and grandfather used natural dyes, by Wardle's time this ancient practice had been superseded by the adoption of modern chemical dyes.

In the mid-1870s, Morris and Wardle worked closely together to revive the art of natural dyestuffs. Both men admired the rich colours in Indian printed fabrics, which were still produced in this way. The British had restricted the export of chemical dyes into India, inadvertently protecting the use of natural dyes. After some early successes, Wardle began to print Morris & Co. cottons commercially.

Morris regularly travelled to Leek to check on progress and to work the dye vats. Indigo blue was the most difficult dye to perfect and around this time his hands were 'habitually and unwashably blue'. Increasingly frustrated with the lack of progress, Morris eventually started looking for his own workshop but the early cottons continued to be printed by Wardle's company into the 20th century.

block-printed cotton, 29.5 x 23 cm (repeat)

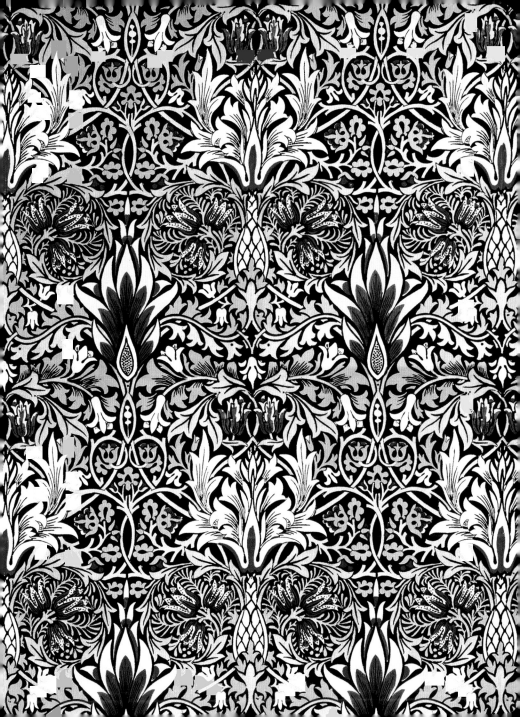

'Ever since I can remember, I was a great devourer of books.'

John Gerard's *Herball*, 1636

Even as a young boy, Morris was fascinated by nature and knew the names of many different plants and flowers. Between 1840 and 1848, when the family lived at Woodford Hall, Essex, the children each had their own little garden to tend. The library contained a copy of Gerard's *Herball* which Morris studied as a child.

First published in 1597, the *Herball* is a reference book, listing where plants grow, what they look like and what they can be used for. Some species would have been familiar to Morris from his countryside rambles, but the book also includes plants from across the world: tobacco from Peru, potatoes from Virginia, an Indian fig tree and a Caribbean plantain.

The Madder plant illustrated was used to make red dye. Unfortunately for Morris, the dye recipe was not included. Traditionally dyeing was a very secretive industry. The best recipes were closely guarded and passed on verbally from craftsman to craftsman.

paper, 33.4 x 21.3 cm leaf

Acquired with the assistance of the V&A Purchase Grant Fund.

CHAP. 460.   Of Madder.

THere is but one kinde of Madder only which is manured or set for vse, but if all those that are like it in leaues and manner of growing were referred thereto, there should be many sorts, as Goose-grasse, soft Cliuer, our Ladies Bedstraw, Woodroofe, and Crosse-wort; all which are like to Madder in leaues, and therefore thought to be wilde kindes thereof.

1 *Rubia tinctorum.*
Red Madder.

2 *Rubia sylvestris.*
Wilde Madder.

Printing textiles at Merton Abbey, late 19th century

In this photograph, the printer positions the woodblock face down onto a length of cotton. He uses a mallet to tap down the block, to ensure the colour transfers evenly. A mobile trolley on tracks holds all his equipment and behind him a length of printed cotton hangs to dry.

Morris had long held an ambition to dye and print his own textiles. In 1881 he set up a workshop at Merton Abbey, Surrey. The River Wandle ran through the site, providing the essential supply of clean, running water for textile manufacture.

Block-printing textiles by hand was a time-consuming and repetitive process. Each colour had to be printed separately and left to dry before the next colour was added. Although the job looks quite monotonous, working conditions and pay were above average for the time.

Morris & Co. tried to stand out from its competitors by advertising the skill and labour that went into its products. This photograph was used to illustrate one of the Firm's trade catalogues in the early 1900s.

'The setting of the blue-vat is a ticklish job, and requires more experience than any other dyeing process.'

Brother Rabbit, design registered 1882

Morris spent years experimenting to achieve rich and lasting shades of blue. He favoured indigo, a plant dye found across the globe. This historic dye had an 'additional touch of fascination' for Morris because it was notoriously difficult to work with.

The blue colour only forms when the fabric is lifted out of the vat and comes into contact with the air. Morris often entertained visitors to Merton by dipping their handkerchiefs into the dye vat, lifting them out and watching them turn blue as if by magic.

Unlike other colours, which can be printed directly onto the cloth, indigo requires a different, more challenging technique. To create this sample of *Brother Rabbit*, the entire length of cotton was first dyed dark blue (the colour of the background) in the dye vat. The cloth was then block-printed with a bleaching agent, which removes some of the blue dye, leaving behind a lighter shade to form the pattern.

block-printed cotton, 33.5 x 23 cm (repeat)

Medway printing block, late 19th century

The continual thump of the woodblocks was one of the most characteristic sounds of the workshops at Merton Abbey. The blocks were cut by Alfred and later James Barrett, specialists based in Bethnal Green. Morris had acquired first-hand experience of the technique when he cut over fifty blocks for his planned edition of *The Earthly Paradise*. This knowledge informed his designs, which he annotated with detailed instructions for the block-cutters.

The blocks were carefully constructed from layers of wood glued together. The top pearwood layer was chiselled away to create the design in relief. Large areas of the surface were sometimes filled in with felt to ensure an even application of colour. Metal strips and pins were inserted for fine detail.

The most complex designs required over thirty blocks to complete. Brass tacks on the corners were used to line up the blocks. Each left a small dot on the surface of the fabric, showing where the next block should be placed.

fruitwood and felt, 46 x 32 cm

Chrysanthemum wallpaper design, 1877

The design is built up of two layers: a background of yellow scrolling foliage overlaid with meandering stems. The veining on the leaves and petals gives a sense of three-dimensionality, which is held in check by the flat pattern below. Morris insisted on a degree of abstraction in his designs, arguing that a realistic depiction of nature was ill suited to the flat surface of a wall.

This complex wallpaper is one of the few Morris & Co. papers to admit the influence of Japanese design, much admired in London's fashionable circles at the time. An even more elaborate lacquered version, with leaves of 'bright bronze green', was used at 1 Holland Park, home to Alexander Ionides, Greek merchant and patron of the arts.

Morris & Co. papers were block-printed by the highly respected firm of Jeffrey & Co., Islington. The quality was so consistent that there was no need to consider in-house production.

pencil and watercolour on paper, 101.3 x 67.3 cm

Artichoke and *Sunflower* tiles, early 1870s

The celebrated ceramic artist William De Morgan started his career working with Morris as a stained glass artist. He realised that the iridescent stain of silver, which was used on the back of stained glass windows, could be reproduced on the glazed surface of a pot or tile to give a similar effect to the ancient ceramic lustre wares of Persia, Italy and Spain. The ruby red tiles are early examples of his work. The two-tone sunflower is more accomplished than the thick, slightly bubbled artichoke.

Morris and De Morgan were lifelong friends and collaborated closely. Their approach to design was so in tune that it is not known which of these tiles were designed by Morris, and which by De Morgan. De Morgan regularly fired Morris's tile designs for him. He was also one of the select few manufacturers whose wares Morris stocked in his shop and recommended to the Firm's clients.

Blue and white tiles were also popular and Morris used the artichoke design in this colour scheme for his own fireplace at Kelmscott Manor, Gloucestershire.

hand-painted earthenware tiles, 15.3 x 15.3 cm each

Acquired with the assistance of the Friends of the WMG.

Point-paper design for
Dove and Rose woven fabric, 1879

At Merton Abbey, Morris installed hand-operated jacquard looms, which partly automated the weaving process. Large orders were sub-contracted to companies that used steam-powered looms. Morris welcomed technological progress that genuinely saved repetitive labour without compromising the quality of the final product. He believed that 'it is the allowing of machines to be our masters and not our servants that so injures the beauty of life nowadays'.

Weaving a pattern is a more complex process than printing. To weave the *Dove and Rose* textile, Morris's original design was painted on point-paper. This was used to make a series of punch cards, which were fed into the loom and controlled the production of the pattern. Morris felt uneasy about subjecting his employees to the 'deafening clatter' of the weaving shed, but accepted it as a necessary evil to produce fine fabrics in silk and wool.

pencil and watercolour on paper, 118 x 51.5 cm

'To us pattern-designers, Persia has become a holy land, for there in the process of time our art was perfected'

Design for *Persian Brocatel*, c.1890

This extremely expensive woven silk was described in the Firm's catalogue as 'the most sumptuous material woven on Merton Abbey looms'. It was originally designed for Stanmore Hall, Middlesex, home to the oil tycoon William Knox D'Arcy. The decoration of Stanmore Hall was one of the most opulent and unrestrained commissions the Firm ever undertook.

By this date, Morris was increasingly distracted by his involvement in politics and heritage conservation. Many of the designs for Stanmore were delegated to John Henry Dearle, a talented employee who became artistic director of the Firm after Morris's death. Dearle readily absorbed the house style and in the past many of his designs have been attributed to Morris. Both men drew inspiration from historic textiles, and in this example the ogee-shaped pattern and palmette motifs clearly show a Middle Eastern influence.

pencil and watercolour on paper, 102.2 x 68.6 cm

*'a perfect hanging for a
medieval castle or mansion'*

Peacock and Dragon, designed 1878

Morris favoured using fabrics as wall-coverings in preference
to wallpapers, which he once described as 'makeshifts for
cheapness' sake'. The repeat of this design was so large (over
a metre tall) that a very spacious room was required to display
it to full advantage. It proved popular at home and abroad,
and was bought by clients in the US, Canada and Australia.

In the late 1870s, Morris wrote to a friend, 'I am studying
birds now to see if I can't get some of them into my next
design'. A number of patterns incorporating pairs of birds
followed, including this example with squawking peacocks
and ferocious dragons. The curved form of the birds has been
cleverly utilised to give shape and structure to the design.

The arrangement of the birds recalls the Sicilian silks that
Morris studied in the South Kensington Museum (now the
Victoria and Albert Museum). The colour scheme is noticeably
different to his earlier work and reflects his increasing interest
in Islamic art. As an acknowledged authority on historic world
textiles, Morris advised the South Kensington Museum on
many major acquisitions including the Ardabil carpet.

woven woollen fabric, 109 x 90 cm (repeat)

*'To apply art to useful wares…
is not a frivolity, but a part of
the serious business of life.'*

Peacock and Bird carpet, 1880s

In Victorian Britain it was fashionable to collect Persian carpets and Morris was no exception. In 1876, he described his latest purchase as one that will 'make you feel as if you were in the Arabian nights'. However, Morris was not content to simply admire historic examples and set himself the challenge of learning to hand-knot carpets.

In the Middle East this craft had been practised for centuries but in Britain Morris had to start from scratch. He first experimented by making small rugs at the family home in Hammersmith. The new workshops at Merton Abbey provided space to set up larger looms and Morris & Co. produced a spectacular range of hand-knotted carpets.

Morris chose to use the Turkish or Symmetrical knot, appropriate for bold designs not fine detail. He employed young women to undertake the work because he thought their smaller fingers were more suited to the task.

woollen pile with a cotton warp, 410 x 410 cm

Acquired with the assistance of The Monument Trust.

Quest for the Holy Grail, 1886

Morris and Burne-Jones both played an important role in the 19th century revival of the legends of King Arthur and the Knights of the Round Table. At university, they spent hours reading aloud their favourite medieval version of the story, Sir Thomas Malory's *Morte D'Arthur*. Burne-Jones once commented, 'Lord! How that San Graal story is ever in my mind and thoughts continually. Was ever anything in the world beautiful as that is beautiful!' In their designs for the Firm they returned to the Arthurian legends time and time again.

This stained glass design was for a more personal use. Burne-Jones depicted four scenes from the quest for the Holy Grail for the windows of his country retreat at Rottingdean, Sussex. In the first panel, Lancelot is prevented from seeing the Grail because of his adulterous love for Queen Guenevere, wife of King Arthur. The angel holding the Grail, a sacred cup symbolising truth, turns his back on the two lovers as they are not 'pure of heart'.

watercolour, ink, Chinese white and gold on paper, 58.2 x 46 cm

how lancelot sought the sangreal and might not see it because
his eyes were blinded by such love as dwelleth in kings houses

'The noblest of the weaving arts is tapestry, in which there is nothing mechanical: it may be looked upon as a mosaic of pieces of colour made up of dyed threads'

Woodpecker tapestry, 1885

Morris first encountered antique tapestries as a child in Queen Elizabeth I's hunting lodge in Epping Forest: 'How well I remember as a boy my first acquaintance with a room hung with faded greenery…and the impression of romance it made upon me'. Years later, he acquired a small loom and taught himself the weaving technique. His first attempt took 516 hours to complete and was so important to him that he kept a diary recording his progress.

This tapestry was woven at Merton Abbey using naturally dyed yarns. Morris's design is inspired by a Classical legend from Ovid's *Metamorphoses*. In this tale, King Picus is transformed into a woodpecker by the sorceress Circe when he refuses her sexual advances.

woven with wool on cotton warp, 287 x 150 cm
Acquired with the assistance of the V&A Purchase Grant Fund.

Photographic cartoon, c.1890–91

In the 1890s the Firm embarked on its most ambitious tapestry commission, a series of panels illustrating the quest for the Holy Grail. These monumental hangings were created for the dining room of Stanmore Hall, Middlesex.

Burne-Jones designed the figures in the six narrative panels. The initial drawings, which were less than fifteen inches high, were enlarged photographically. Burne-Jones made any final alterations directly to the surface of these photographs. The designs were then sent to the weavers who used them to trace the outlines onto the warp (fixed vertical) threads.

This photograph is a detail from the first panel, in which the Knights of the Round Table are summoned to seek the Grail. Sir Bors and Sir Palomydes turn to face the 'strange damsel' who has brought news of the quest. In the 19th century, tapestry was a very unusual and expensive method of wall decoration but these panels were so admired that several other clients ordered versions from the Firm.

watercolour, gouache and ink over photographic image, 207.5 x 85 cm

Conserved with the assistance of The Mercers' Company.

Velveteen sample book, 1890s

Morris was an astute businessman, continually seeking new markets and working to expand the Firm's product range. In the early years, commissions for stained glass and church furnishings were the main source of income. As demand for these goods fell in the 1870s, Morris understood the need to diversify.

He decided to expand the range of domestic furnishings — especially wallpapers and fabrics — to appeal to a wider public. The Firm opened a showroom on Oxford Street, in the heart of the fashionable West End. Sample books like this were available for customers to browse, just as we do today.

Velveteen became a fashionable furnishing fabric in the 1880s. As early as 1877 Morris recognised its potential: 'we could have a good trade in velvets and serges if we could get the colours good and fast'.

31.1 x 21.6 cm (closed)

Acquired with the assistance of the MGC/V&A Purchase Grant Fund.

Interior of a Morris & Co. showroom, c.1917

Morris & Co. developed a distinct brand identity that made its products instantly recognisable. In efforts to influence public taste, a lot of care was taken in planning the layout of the showroom. Attractive room settings helped clients visualise how to combine different products in their own homes.

The large wallpaper swatch book in the foreground shows the *Daisy* design, a consistent bestseller from the 1860s until the closure of the Firm in 1940. A tapestry, designed by Burne-Jones, enlivens the wall above the fireplace. Towards the back of the shop, stacks of sample books and photographs were available to show clients the full range of designs.

At the time this watercolour was painted, the Firm had long employed professional shop staff. In the early days, the atmosphere was more informal and one client remembered being served by Morris himself: 'someone came from above with his hair on end and in a nonchalant way began to show me one or two of his curios'.

published in Morris & Co. *Change of Address* brochure

'Lo, silken my garden & silken my sky,
And silken the apple boughs hanging on high.
All wrought by the worm in the peasant carle's cot
On the mulberry leafage when summer was hot.'

The Fruit Garden, early 1890s

Morris's younger daughter, May, became head of the Firm's embroidery department in 1885. She ran the workshop from her home at 8 Hammersmith Terrace, and supervised a team of embroideresses, including Lily Yeats, sister of the poet W.B. Yeats.

This design was used for a portière, a heavy curtain that hung across the door. It was one of May's most accomplished works and was very popular in the 1890s. The embroidery was sold as a kit, complete with Morris & Co. dyed yarns, to be stitched at home. Alternatively, for a higher price, the embroidery could be purchased fully worked.

Finely executed watercolours like this were often shown to prospective clients in the shop and this example is inscribed with the Oxford Street address. Stock designs could be adapted and versions of this one exist with inscriptions from Morris's poem, *The Flowering Orchard*.

watercolour, ink and graphite on paper, 33.3 x 20.4 cm

Battye embroidery, c.1900

This idiosyncratic design was commissioned by Mrs. Battye, one of the Firm's regular clients, in the 1890s. One of the largest hangings May Morris designed, it was expertly stitched by the women of the Battye family.

May often included embroidered inscriptions in her designs, usually taken from her father's poetry. In this case, the inclusion of over fifteen different mottoes and proverbs was probably requested by Mrs Battye, along with the family's coats-of-arms. The overall effect is a celebration of nature: exotic coloured birds fly in and out of the trees and small forest animals nestle in the foreground. The surface of the hessian is entirely covered in stitch work, an unusual feature among May's designs, which usually incorporated unworked sections.

In addition to her work for Morris & Co., May promoted embroidery as a serious art form. She published a guide for beginners, *Decorative Needlework* (1893), taught at several art schools and gave a lecture tour in the United States, 1909–10.

silk on hessian canvas, 188 x 296 cm

Conserved with the assistance of The Textile Society.

'Apart from the desire to produce beautiful things, the leading passion of my life has been and is hatred of modern civilisation.'

Socialist flyer, 1887

Morris came from a privileged background and is famous for running a successful commercial business. As he got older, however, he became increasingly uncomfortable about the divide between rich and poor. In the 1880s he acted on this unease and took on a leading role in the early Socialist Movement.

A committed open-air speaker, Morris travelled all over Britain to rally support. He visited the East End of London, speaking in parks, coffee houses and on street corners. He clashed with the authorities on more than one occasion and was even briefly arrested for disorderly conduct. To help spread the word he edited and largely funded *Commonweal*, a socialist newspaper.

Walter Crane designed the Socialist League masthead, bearing the slogan 'Agitate Educate Organize'. Morris aimed to spread socialist ideas amongst the workers and bring about a revolution. In the early days, he was hopeful that radical change could be achieved in his own lifetime.

printed handbill, 20.3 x 13 cm

NO COERCION!

VICTORIA PARK, SATURDAY MAY 21, 1887.

No. 10 Platform.

Chairman—H. A. BARKER.

SPECIAL RESOLUTION.

" *That this meeting expresses its deep abhorrence of the Coercive Measures levelled against the Irish nation, and is of opinion that, the Land Question being at the root of the Irish troubles, no political change can have permanent value unless accompanied by, or be in the direction of the abolition of Landlordism in Ireland; and is further of opinion that the Irish nation should be left free to settle with the landlords without any restriction whatever from the English Parliament.*"

SPEAKERS.

ANNIE BESANT.	WILLIAM MORRIS.
G. B. SHAW.	H. H. SPARLING.
H. DAVIS. J. LANE.	C. W. WADE.

The **Commonweal**, *Socialist Journal* (1d. weekly), and *pamphlets on Socialism, may be had from the Secretary of the* SOCIALIST LEAGUE, *13 Farringdon Road, London, E.C.*

*'How can I ask working-men passing
up and down these hideous streets
day to day to care about beauty?'*

Socialist banner, c.1890s

When Morris and his comrades attended rallies and marches, they carried banners to identify their political allegiance. The imagery on this example has been borrowed from Burne-Jones's illustration to Morris's socialist novel *The Dream of John Ball*. Ball was a radical priest who helped to stir up the Peasants' Revolt of 1381. He argued that all men were created equal, hence the invocation of Adam and Eve in the Garden of Eden. His words were adopted by socialists in their fight to end the class system.

Morris experienced mixed reactions from his friends when he became politically radical. Many were shocked at his attack on privilege and private property. Others, including his daughters, joined up in support.

Throughout the decade of his most strenuous political engagement, Morris continued to run his design business. Although he delegated many day-to-day tasks, these were also the years when a whole range of new manufacturing processes was introduced at Merton Abbey.

painted and embroidered silk, 168 x 91 cm

Conserved with the assistance of The Kathy Callow Trust.

SOCIALISM

FELLOWSHIP

BROTHERHOOD

WHAN ADAM DELVED
AND EVE SPAN
WHO WAS THEN
THE GENTLEMAN

News From Nowhere,
Kelmscott Press edition, 1893

In the 1890s Morris established the Kelmscott Press, realising his longheld ambition to print fine books with a 'definite claim to beauty'. He was involved in every aspect of design and production, from creating new typefaces to carefully selecting the paper and ink.

In his utopian fiction, *News From Nowhere*, Morris imagines a future in which capitalism, heavy industry and government have all been swept away. The countryside has taken over the towns and cities, which are now pleasant, green and healthy places to live. Resources are shared communally and people freely choose how to spend their time; work is synonymous with pleasure.

This edition is illustrated with a woodcut of his country retreat, Kelmscott Manor in Gloucestershire. Morris was deeply attached to this old house by the Thames. The building's features, be it the weathered stone walls or the slate roof, took on almost human characteristics. He liked to think that the house had 'grown up out of the soil and the lives of those that lived upon it'.

paper with half-holland binding, 20.6 x 14 cm leaf

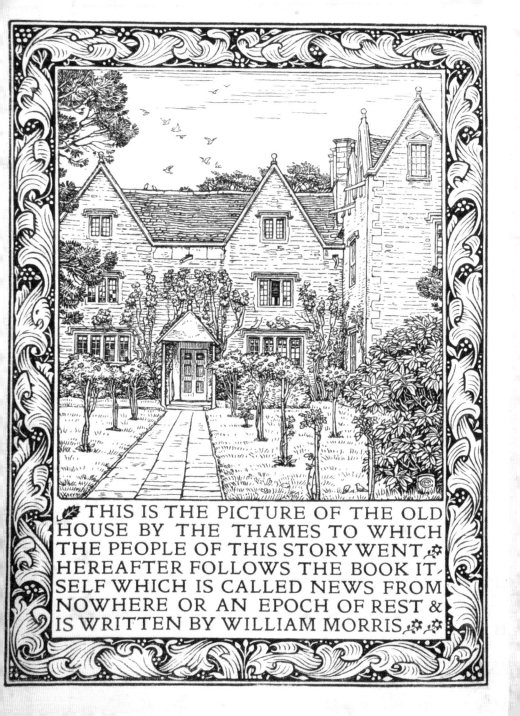

THIS IS THE PICTURE OF THE OLD
HOUSE BY THE THAMES TO WHICH
THE PEOPLE OF THIS STORY WENT
HEREAFTER FOLLOWS THE BOOK IT
SELF WHICH IS CALLED NEWS FROM
NOWHERE OR AN EPOCH OF REST &
IS WRITTEN BY WILLIAM MORRIS

Pilgrim and the Heart of the Rose, c.1874–82

The legend of *The Romaunt of the Rose* inspired the Firm's largest scheme of figurative embroidery. Commissioned by the ironmaster Sir Isaac Lowthian Bell, the frieze decorated the walls of his dining room at Rounton Grange, Yorkshire. Measuring over 20 metres in total, the panels were expertly stitched by the client's wife and daughter, Margaret and Florence Bell. Burne-Jones drew the figures and most of the background detail, to which Morris contributed as well.

The story comes from a 13th century French poem and part of its translation into Middle English is attributed to Chaucer. It is an allegorical tale about the quest for courtly and philosophical love. After a treacherous journey in which the Pilgrim must overcome many dangers, he is finally united with his love, a beautiful maiden enveloped by a rose bush. This panel shows the final scene.

linen embroidered with silks, wools and metal thread, 96.5 x 126 cm

The Heart of the Rose, c.1889

As well as designing *The Romaunt of the Rose* embroideries for the Firm, Burne-Jones treated the same subject in his own work. This chalk study shows a different composition for the final scene in the legend. The pilgrim, with his back to the viewer, is guided by the winged figure of love. He is led into the presence of his beloved, a beautiful maiden seated in a rose bush.

This study for an oil painting is a good example of how Burne-Jones's fine art and decorative work were closely interwoven. As an idea developed, it could find expression in many different forms. The same subject was also adapted for tapestry and as an illustration in the famous *Kelmscott Chaucer*.

charcoal and coloured chalks on brown paper,
84 x 130 cm

'This is the Great Story of the North, which should be to all our race what the Tale of Troy was to the Greeks...'

Sigurd the Volsung,
Kelmscott Press edition, 1898

The Norse sagas, full of bloodthirsty family feuds and epic battles, are not for the faint-hearted. Morris admired them greatly and worked with the Icelandic scholar Eiríkr Magnússon to translate them into English. He travelled to Iceland and trekked across the landscape visiting the ancient saga sites. In 1876, he completed his own poetic version of the Sigurd legend, a work 'he held most highly and wished to be remembered by'.

Morris planned a lavishly illustrated edition of his poem. Unfortunately Burne-Jones, the principal illustrator of the Kelmscott Press, did not share his enthusiasm for the sagas, claiming 'I've no turn for the dramatic'. Nevertheless, he produced two designs, including this depiction of a vaulted hall. The tables are laid for a feast; a great tree grows from the centre of the floor and wild hawks perch amidst the foliage. The book was eventually published two years after Morris's death, just before the Kelmscott Press was disbanded.

paper with vellum binding, 32.2 x 23.5 cm leaf

William Morris giving a weaving demonstration, 1888

As a schoolboy in Birmingham, Burne-Jones entertained his friends by sketching caricatures. He continued this practice throughout his life, often illustrating the letters he sent to his friends. Morris, with his wild curly hair and stout figure, was a favourite subject.

This sketch shows Morris giving a practical demonstration at the first Arts and Crafts Exhibition Society show at the New Gallery in Regent Street. Morris delivered a lecture on tapestry and carpet weaving and the first row of the audience appear in the foreground.

Although gently poking fun at his friend — the waistcoat looks fit to burst — Burne-Jones's drawing captures Morris's hands-on approach to art. Seated at a large loom, weaving the shuttle in and out, Morris's pleasure in his work is evident. Through his involvement with the Arts & Crafts Exhibition Society, Morris influenced younger craftspeople who carried his legacy into the 20th century.

pencil on paper, 22.9 x 17.5 cm

'We sat down at last in a room…which was still hung with old tapestry, originally of no artistic value, but now faded into pleasant grey tones which harmonised thoroughly well with the quiet of the place…'

May Morris at Kelmscott Manor, c.1910

After Morris's death in 1896, his family remained attached to their much-loved country home. May was painted in the tapestry room by her friend, the artist Mary Sloane. She is surrounded by papers, hard at work editing her father's *Collected Works*, which eventually ran to twenty-four volumes. On her lap she holds one of the vellum-bound Kelmscott Press books with the familiar red silk ties.

As well as pursuing an illustrious career in embroidery and teaching, May played a vital role in preserving her father's memory. The task of editing his vast literary output took nine years to complete. She later travelled to Iceland, retracing Morris's steps and trying to experience the landscape as he would have done.

Morris was buried in the churchyard at Kelmscott. The modest tombstone was designed by his friend, Philip Webb, eventually marking the grave of all four family members.

watercolour on paper, 27.3 x 37.5 cm

Chronology

Further Resources

William Morris' Socialist Diary,
ed. Florence Boos, Journeyman, 1985

The Collected Letters of William Morris,
ed. Norman Kelvin, 4 volumes,
Princeton University Press, 1984-1996

William Morris: A Life for Our Time,
Fiona MacCarthy, Faber and Faber, 1994

The Life of William Morris,
John W. Mackail, 2 volumes, Longmans,
Green & Co., 1899

Icelandic Journals,
ed. Magnus Magnusson, Mare's Nest, 1996

*Jane and May Morris: A Biographical Story
1839-1938,*
Jan Marsh, Pandora Press, 1986

The Collected Works of William Morris,
ed. May Morris, 24 volumes, Longmans,
Green & Co, 1910-1915

William Morris Tiles,
Richard and Hilary Myers, Richard Dennis, 1996

William Morris,
ed. Linda Parry, V&A exhibition catalogue,
Philip Wilson Ltd, 1996

William Morris Textiles,
Linda Parry, V&A Publications, rev. ed., 2013

*The Kelmscott Press: A History of
William Morris's Typographical Adventure,*
William S. Peterson, Oxford University Press, 1991

The Stained Glass of William Morris and his Circle,
A. C. Sewter, 2 volumes,
Yale University Press, 1974-1975

News From Nowhere and Other Writings,
ed. Clive Wilmer, Penguin, 1993

All these titles and many more are available to
view in the William Morris Gallery reading room;
open to everyone by appointment.

Kelmscott House: © William Morris Society   Red House: © The National Trust Photo Library

Places to visit

LONDON

William Morris Gallery, Walthamstow

An internationally renowned collection devoted to the life, achievements and legacy of William Morris.
www.wmgallery.org.uk

7 Hammersmith Terrace, Hammersmith

Step inside a late 19th century interior with many Morris & Co. furnishings. The former home of the printer Emery Walker — Morris's friend, collaborator and neighbour.
www.emerywalker.org.uk

De Morgan Centre, Wandsworth

The largest collection of William De Morgan's ceramics displayed alongside paintings by his wife Evelyn.
www.demorgan.org.uk

Kelmscott House, Hammersmith

The William Morris Society now occupies the basement and coach house of Morris's London home. Highlights from the collection include original designs and the Albion Press used by the Kelmscott Press.
www.williammorrissociety.org

Red House, Bexleyheath

Find out where it all began. The house commissioned by Morris, designed by Philip Webb, and decorated by the group of friends.
www.nationaltrust.org.uk/main/w-redhouse

Victoria and Albert Museum, South Kensington

Visit the Green Dining Room decorated by the Firm and find a selection of Morris & Co. designs, furniture, glass, wallpapers and textiles mostly in the British Galleries.
www.vam.ac.uk

Kelmscott Manor:
© Society of Antiquaries of London

FURTHER AFIELD

Birmingham Museum and Art Gallery
A rich collection of Pre-Raphaelite art, Morris & Co. designs and the famous Holy Grail tapestries.
www.bmag.org.uk

Blackwell, Bowness-on-Windermere, Cumbria
An icon of Arts and Crafts architecture, furnished by the Movement's leading designers including Morris & Co.
www.blackwell.org.uk

Cheltenham Art Gallery & Museum, Cheltenham, Gloucestershire
A nationally important collection of Arts and Crafts material and home to the Emery Walker library.
www.artsandcraftsmuseum.org.uk

Court Barn Museum, Chipping Campden, Gloucestershire
Celebrating the Arts and Crafts artists of the Cotswolds, particularly C.R. Ashbee and the Guild of Handicraft.
www.courtbarn.org.uk

Kelmscott Manor, near Lechlade, Gloucestershire
A Grade I listed farmhouse bordering on the river Thames; the Morris family's country retreat and home to a celebrated collection of the work of Morris and Rossetti.
www.kelmscottmanor.org.uk

National Trust
It is a testament to Morris & Co.'s success that so many National Trust properties contain furnishings by the Firm. Look out especially for Wightwick Manor in Wolverhampton with original Morris wallpapers and fabrics, De Morgan tiles and Pre-Raphaelite art. Another highlight is Standen in West Sussex, a showpiece of the Arts & Crafts Movement, designed by Philip Webb.
www.nationaltrust.org.uk

Oxford Union, Oxford
The former Debating Chamber is decorated with Arthurian murals painted in the 1850s by Morris, Rossetti, Burne-Jones and others.
www.oxford-union.org.uk/library/murals

The Stained Glass Museum, Ely
Discover the history and beauty of this ancient craft and the role played by Morris & Co.
www.stainedglassmuseum.com

You Are Magical!

Inspiring Short Stories for Girls About
Self-Confidence, Friendship, Love and Inner Strength

AVIA JOYCE

Thank you for buying our book!

If you find this storybook fun and useful, we would be very grateful if you could post a short review on Amazon! Your support does make a difference and we read every review personally.

If you would like to leave a review, just head on over to this book's Amazon page and click "Write a customer review."

Thank you for your support!